MIRACLE ON 34TH STREET

A Hollywood Classic

MIRACLE ON 34TH STREET

A Hollywood Classic

Sarah Parker Danielson

SMITHMARK

Copyright © 1993 Brompton Books Corp.

All rights reserved. No part of this publication may be reproduced, stored in a retrieval system or transmitted in any form by any means, electronic, mechanical, photocopying or otherwise, without first obtaining written permission of the copyright owner.

This edition published in 1994 by SMITHMARK Publishers Inc., 16 East 32nd Street New York, New York 10016

SMITHMARK books are available for bulk purchase for sales promotion and premium use. For details write or telephone the Manager of Special Sales, SMITHMARK Publishers Inc., 16 East 32nd Street, New York, NY 10016. (212) 532-6600.

Produced by Brompton Books Corp., 15 Sherwood Place Greenwich, CT 06830

ISBN 0-8317-4284-4

Printed in China

10 9 8 7 6 5 4 3 2

Designed by Ruth DeJauregui

All photos appear courtesy of American Graphic Systems Picture Archives with the following exceptions:
Wisconsin Center for Film & Theater Research 24-25, 80-81, 86-87

Page 1: Natalie Wood and the other child stars of **Miracle on 34th Street** gather round Edmund Gwenn, who played Kris Kringle.

Page 2: The central characters of **Miracle on 34th Street** — Susan and Kris Kringle.

MIRACLE ON 34TH STREET

CAST

Susan Walker	Natalie Wood
Doris Walker	Maureen O'Hara
Fred Gailey	John Payne
Kris Kringle	Edmund Gwenn
Judge Henry X Harper	Gene Lockhart
Thomas Mara	Jerome Cowan
Mr Shellhammer	Philip Tonge
Mr Sawyer	Porter Hall
Dr Pierce	James Seay
RH Macy	Harry Antrim
Alfred	Alvin Greenman
Charlie	William Frawley
Lady in Macy's	Thelma Ritter
Mrs Shellhammer	Lela Bliss

Director	George Seaton
Producer	William Perlberg
Screenplay	George Seaton
Cinematography	Charles Clark and Lloyd Ahern
Editor	Robert Simpson
Music	Cyril Mockridge

Based on the story by Valentine Davies

INTRODUCTION

There is no surer sign that the holiday season has arrived than the appearance of **Miracle on 34th Street** on television for its annual Christmas run. This modern day fable about faith revolves around an old man named Kris Kringle who believes he is Santa Claus. In his struggle to keep the meaning of Christmas alive year round, Kris teaches a skeptical little girl how to be a child and in the process convinces her that he really is Santa Claus. By the film's conclusion most of the audience is convinced, too. Along the way, he turns Macy's department store upside down with his unorthodox approach to marketing and even has Mr Macy and Mr Gimbel shaking hands as they bend over backwards sending their customers to each other's stores.

Miracle on 34th Street opens with a New York tradition: Macy's Annual Thanksgiving parade, the official beginning of the Christmas shopping season. With the hustle and bustle of Manhattan as a backdrop, the script moves along at a quick pace (only 96 minutes) culminating in a court-room scene filled with humor and irony. Santa may be on trial for lunacy, but he hasn't lost his sense of humor. It is, in fact, director George Seaton's ability to poke fun at our human foibles that keeps the film from becoming overly sentimental. **Miracle on 34th Street** is filled with devilishly funny portraits of human nature. Mr Sawyer, for example, is a bundle of neuroses; Mrs Shellhammer, in only thirty seconds, personifies the classic society matron, drunkenly declaring it would be 'simply charming' to have Santa Claus as a house guest; and Mr Macy and Mr Gimbel are the perfect 'money-grubbing profiteers.'

This is not to say the film doesn't have its share of heartwarming moments. Kris singing with the little girl in Dutch or Dr Pierce dumbstruck at the sight of his new X-ray machine are but two examples of scenes guaranteed to raise a lump in the throat of even the most hardened Scrooge.

Facing page: Judging from the look on her face, Susan (Natalie Wood) is a bit skeptical about Christmas and Santa Claus.

Director George Seaton also wrote the screenplay, and won an Academy Award for his efforts. Before turning to directing Seaton was a screenwriter, most notably for the Marx Brothers, an experience which undoubtedly honed his comedic skills. Seaton based his screenplay on a story by Valentine Davies, who first told Seaton of his idea while the two were vacationing with their wives in Nevada. Eighteen months later Seaton had a rough draft using the pseudonyms Tracy's and Trimbell's for Macy's and Gimbel's. He approached the actual stores and both agreed that Seaton could use their names even though the stores were presented in a less than favorable light.

Miracle on 34th Street stars Natalie Wood as six-year-old Susan Walker, Maureen O'Hara as her mother, and John Payne as the neighbor who wins Susie's friendship and her mother's heart. The film's most unforgettable character, however, is 72-year-old Edmund Gwenn. With a twinkle in his eyes and a spring to his step, Gwenn crafted a delightful Kris Kringle and earned himself an Academy Award for Best Supporting Actor.

The strong supporting cast includes Porter Hall as the paranoid Mr Sawyer, Gene Lockhart as the judge faced with the burdensome task of ruling on Kris Kringle's sanity and William Frawley as the judge's wily political advisor. Even the bit players — Thelma Ritter as the lady in Macy's or Lela Bliss as Mrs Shellhammer — make the most of their brief scenes.

Though its setting is the Christmas season, the film's message is a simple one applicable year round: Life's intangibles are what make living worthwhile. As Fred Gailey points out, what really matters are the things that Kris Kringle stands for — hope, joy, kindness and love. That the characters in the film come to understand the meaning of these intangibles is the miracle on 34th Street.

Facing page: John Payne's charm and good looks made him a favorite with female movie-goers of the 1940s.

Above: This original movie poster for **Miracle on 34th Street** appears to be advertising a love story between Maureen O'Hara and John Payne rather than a Christmas story starring Edmund Gwenn as Santa Claus.

Facing page: Off screen, Natalie Wood was more willing to be a child than Susan, the character she played. Here, she and Edmund Gwenn get acquainted with a puppy.

MIRACLE ON 34TH STREET

Miracle on 34th Street opens with a scene of the bustling streets of New York City. It's Thanksgiving Day and Macy's annual parade is about to begin. Immediately the viewer is transported to New York City and can almost feel the nip in the air and the excitement that signals the start of the holiday season. As is characteristic of 20th Century-Fox productions during Hollywood's golden era, **Miracle on 34th Street** has a visual gloss to it.

From the back we see an older man (Edmund Gwenn) jauntily strolling down the street, cane in hand. He pauses at a shop window where a shopkeeper is putting the final touches on a Christmas display. The man in the shop, however, has got it all wrong. 'You're making a mistake with the reindeer,' the passerby tells him. It seems Cupid is where Blitzen should be, and Donner doesn't have the correct number of prongs on his antlers. The shopkeeper shakes his head and the stranger moves on, singing 'Jingle Bells' to himself as he makes his way to where Macy's Thanksgiving Parade is about to begin. He encounters the hired Santa — who has been drinking. The older man is outraged — 'You're a disgrace to the traditions of Christmas and I refuse to have you malign me in this fashion,' he tells the drunken Santa as he goes off to find Mrs Walker, the parade's organizer. Reluctantly, he agrees to fill in for Santa so the children won't be disappointed. As it turns out he's the best Santa Claus Macy's has ever had, but that should come as no surprise since he claims he is Kris Kringle.

Edmund Gwenn had been acting for decades when he finally earned fame and an Academy Award for Best Supporting Actor for his performance as Kris Kringle. Born in Glamorgan, Wales in 1875, Gwenn appeared in numerous stage productions in London's West End, making the transition to film in 1916. Best known for his performance as Macy's Santa Claus in **Miracle on 34th Street**, Gwenn's other film credits include **The Real Thing at Last** (1916), **Money for Nothing** (1932), **Sylvia Scarlett** (1936), **Parnell** (1937), **Pride and Prejudice** (1940), **Lassie Come Home** (1943), **Bonzo Goes to College** (1952) and **The Trouble with Harry** (1955). *At right* we see Gwenn minus Santa's beard.

Right: From an apartment above, six-year-old Susan Walker (Natalie Wood), the daughter of the parade organizer, is watching the parade with her new neighbor Fred Gailey (John Payne). Assuming that she is a typical six-year-old, Mr Gailey tries to engage her in conversation about the characters in the parade. Susan, however, has a 'no nonsense' approach to life. She does not waste her time thinking about giants or fairy tales, which her mother thinks are silly, and she certainly does not believe in Santa Claus. Not wanting to fill her daughter's head with 'myths and legends' Doris Walker has explained to Susan that Santa Claus is only a fictional character, not a real person at all.

Right: Doris Walker (Maureen O'Hara) stops by Mr Gailey's apartment to pick up her daughter.

Maureen O'Hara was born Maureen Fitzsimmons near Dublin, Ireland. She began her career playing ingenue roles with Dublin's Abbey Players, making her screen debut in London in 1938. The following year she left for Hollywood, landing the role of Esmerelda in **The Hunchback of Notre Dame** (1939). The turning point in her career came in 1941 when director John Ford, who was then America's leading director, cast her in **How Green Was My Valley** (1941). Her association with Ford would continue throughout her career in such films as **Rio Grande** (1950), **The Quiet Man** (1952) and **The Long Gray Line** (1955).

Maureen O'Hara's other films include **Buffalo Bill** (1944), **Father Was a Fullback** (1944), **Tripoli** (1950), **Lady Godiva** (1955), **The Wings of Eagles** (1957), **Our Man in Havana** (1959), **McLintock!** (1963) and **Big Jake** (1971).

Left: **Miracle on 34th Street** is also a love story, and this scene sets up the romance between Doris Walker and Fred Gailey. Over coffee, Fred confesses to Doris that while he is genuinely fond of Susan, he had really been trying to meet her. Doris, however, has been disappointed in love before and is guarded. Her comment 'I think we should be realistic and completely truthful with our children and not have them growing up believing in lots of legends and myths like Santa Claus, for example' reveals as much about her personal life as it does about her views on parenting. As the film progresses, Fred will discover that he needs a little assistance from Santa Claus.

Maureen O'Hara was at her best as the lone woman in a man's world (even in this film she played an executive in the male dominated business world). She often played a stubborn, determined character with a temper to match her fiery red hair. A favorite of director John Ford, she was frequently paired with John Wayne in relationships that were characterized by shouting and cursing until she finally fell into his arms.

Facing page: As part of his plan to get to know Doris better, Fred has suggested to Susan that she encourage her mother to invite him over for Thanksgiving dinner. When the dialogue doesn't go quite as he had planned, a guileless Susan wants to know if she asked all right. 'Susie, honey, you asked just right,' Fred tells her, for he got the result he was hoping for — an invitation to dinner.

The daughter of Russian immigrants, Natalie Wood was born Natasha Gurdin. She was five when she appeared in her first film, **Happy Land** (1943), which was made in her hometown of Santa Rosa, California, a small town about an hour's drive north of San Francisco. Though it was only a bit part, she made such an impression on the director, Irving Pichel, that he later called Natalie's mother, Marie Gurdin, and asked her to bring Natalie to Hollywood to audition for a role in **Tomorrow is Forever** (1946) with Orson Welles and Claudette Colbert. Determined to make her daughter a star, Mrs Gurdin immediately moved the family south to Hollywood. Natalie failed her screen test, but her mother persuaded Pichel to arrange for a second test. She passed, and Pichel renamed her Natalie Wood, after his friend Sam Wood, the director.

Pichel directed Natalie again in her third film, **The Bride Wore Boots** (1946) with Barbara Stanwyck. He was quite fond of her and reputedly asked her mother if he could adopt her. Though his request was denied he remained friends with mother and daughter, and helped to make Natalie's childhood as normal as possible — an often difficult task in Hollywood.

Facing page: Natalie Wood rehearses at the piano. **Miracle on 34th Street** was Natalie Wood's fourth film, and it was already clear that she was going to be a star.

Unlike many child stars, Wood's career successfully continued into adulthood. She was nominated for Academy Awards for **Rebel Without a Cause** (1955), **Splendor in the Grass** (1961) and **Love with the Proper Stranger** (1963). Wood married actor Robert Wagner, divorced him and later remarried him. She had just completed **Brainstorm** with Christopher Walken when she drowned off the coast of California in November 1981. Her other films include **Marjorie Morningstar** (1960), **West Side Story** (1961), **Gypsy** (1962), **Sex and the Single Girl** (1964), **Inside Daisy Clover** (1966), **Bob & Carol & Ted & Alice** (1969) and **The Last Married Couple in America** (1979).

24

Left: After the parade, Santa waves to the cheering crowd, proclaiming 'You'll find toys of all kinds at Macy's.' Having miraculously appeared on the scene, the mysterious stranger—whose name we will soon learn is Kris Kringle—agrees to become Macy's full-time Santa. On Kris' first day on the job, the manager of the toy department, Mr Shellhammer, gives him a list of overstocked toys that Santa needs to promote. Kris, however, has had plenty of practice being Santa and ignores his instructions. Director George Seaton has wasted no time in conveying the message of the film, as Kris Kringle decries the commercialization of Christmas.

Macy's hadn't counted on its newest Santa doing things his own way rather than Macy's way. Instead of encouraging parents to buy toys that happen to be in stock at Macy's, Santa sends them to a store where they can find what they are looking for, even if that means sending the customer to arch rival Gimbels.

Thelma Ritter (*facing page*) played the mother who was amazed that Macy's would send its customers to a competitor. Macy's goodwill attitude has so impressed her that she vows she'll do all her shopping at Macy's from here on out. This was Ritter's first film role, and though she is on screen for approximately one minute, her wisecracking attitude set the tone for her career. A highly regarded character actress, Ms Ritter has been nominated for six Academy Awards.

Left: Though she really doesn't see the point, Susan humors her new friend Mr Gailey and agrees to meet Santa Claus. Susan finds this Santa much better looking than last year's Santa, who had strings attached to his beard, but her views on the existence of Santa Claus remained unchanged. To persuade a doubting Susan that he is indeed Santa Claus, Kris Kringle encourages her to tug on his beard. Much to her surprise, his beard is real.

Natalie Wood's expressions, whether conveying doubt or surprise, are a delight to watch. Irving Pichel, the director who discovered her, considered her a natural.

Left: Santa Claus has no trouble recognizing a skeptic, as he tries to cajole Susan into telling him what she wants for Christmas. Not easily converted, Susan insists that her mother will bring her whatever she needs, 'as long as it's sensible and doesn't cost too much.'

Left: Doris doesn't approve of Susan meeting Santa, fearing that it will create a 'harmful mental conflict' in Susie. Who should Susie believe? Her mother who tells her there is no such person as Santa Claus, or the hundreds of children eagerly waiting to talk to Santa. Doris goes on to explain her views on raising children to Fred:

'By filling them full of fairy tales, they grow up considering life a fantasy instead of a reality. They keep waiting for Prince Charming to come along and when he does, he turns out to be a....'

'We were talking about Susie, not about you,' Fred astutely replies.

While Doris and Fred are talking, Susan has turned back to watch Santa and sees him speaking Dutch with a little girl. To her, this is one more piece of evidence that Kris might really be Santa Claus.

Left: Kris Kringle makes such a convincing Santa Claus that Susan begins to think there really is a Santa Claus. Doris asks Kris to set the record straight—and he does. He really is Santa Claus he tells her. Exasperated, Doris calls for his employee card and is dismayed by what she sees. He identifies himself as Kris Kringle, and claims to be as old as his tongue and a little bit older than his teeth. Furthermore, he names Dasher, Dancer, Prancer, Vixen, Comet, Cupid, Donner and Blitzen as his nearest relatives. Fearful that she is dealing with an insane man, Doris fires him.

Meanwhile, Macy's has been inundated with phone calls, telegrams and letters, and has made front page news with its new found philosophy of putting the customer first. Mr Macy himself is so pleased with the results of this unorthodox method that he wants the philosophy adapted storewide. From this point on, he declares, Macy's 'will be the helpful store, the friendly store, the store with a heart, the store that places public service ahead of profits and consequently we'll make more profits than ever before.'

One of the things that makes **Miracle on 34th Street** such a delightful movie is that it is infused with enough humor and irony to keep it from becoming overly sentimental. Kris, for example, offers a hilarious parody of the psychological test that he'll be given by the store's Mr Sawyer. And when Doris and Mr Shellhammer are debating what to do about Kris, Mr Shellhammer, with understated irony, delivers the following line: 'Maybe he's only a little bit crazy—like painters or composers, or some of those men in Washington.'

Above: Maureen O'Hara and Natalie Wood pose for a behind-the-scenes publicity still.

Facing page: An earlier studio portrait of Maureen O'Hara. With her flaming red hair and bright green eyes, Maureen O'Hara was known as the 'Queen of Technicolor.'

After their meeting with Mr Macy, Doris and Mr Shellhammer are in a quandary over what to do about Kris. They decide to keep him, providing he passes a mental exam administered by the store's Mr Sawyer. While Kris passes his mental exam, he doesn't score any points with Mr Sawyer, who is a bundle of insecurities. Sawyer claims that Kris Kringle has 'latent maniacal tendencies' and will someday become violent. He recommends that Kris be dismissed. Dr Pierce of the Brooks Memorial Home for the Aged, where Kris lives, disagrees with Mr Sawyer's assessment and suggests a compromise: find a place for Kris to live in the city. Doris and Mr Shellhammer agree that having Kris stay at the Shellhammers' while their son is away at school would be ideal—if only they can convince Mrs Shellhammer. To that end, Doris invites Kris to dinner at her house, so that Mr Shellhammer can ply his wife with martinis in order to make her more amenable to the idea of having Santa Claus as a house guest. While at dinner at the Walker's, Kris gets better acquainted with Susan (*right*).

Facing page: In this memorable scene, Kris Kringle gives Susan her first lesson in using her imagination by showing her how to be a monkey.

When Kris questions Susan about what kinds of games she plays with the other children in the building, she tells him that they play silly games. Susan is so indoctrinated with her mother's emphasis on common sense that she won't allow herself to play make believe with the other children. The two engage in a discussion of imagination—which to Susan means seeing things that aren't really there. To Kris, however, the imagination is 'a place all by itself, a separate country.' According to Kris, it's a wonderful place where you can make snowballs in the summer, or drive a great big bus down Fifth Avenue. It's a place where you can be the statue of liberty in the morning and fly south with a flock of geese in the afternoon. Intrigued by his tales of fantasy, Susan becomes a willing pupil as Kris teaches her something every child should know—how to play.

Facing page: Kris and Fred cook up a scheme. After seeing Kris and Susan play together, Fred has a sudden inspiration. Kris can stay at his apartment, thus giving Kris more time to spend with Susan and Doris. Recognizing the beauty of the plan, Kris immediately agrees. Just then Mr Shellhammer calls. After her triple strength martinis, his wife is more than happy to have Santa Claus stay with them.

Overleaf: Susie practices her monkey routine as Kris Kringle and Fred watch with amusement. When people think of **Miracle on 34th Street**, the first thing that comes to mind for many is the image of young Natalie Wood. Whatever the scene, be it when Susan is pulling on Kris' beard, learning how to use her imagination or running through her suburban dream house shouting that Kris really is Santa Claus, Wood's acting was absolutely superb.

Above: John Payne first arrived in Hollywood in 1935 after a brief stint as a vocalist and on stage. A popular leading man of the 1940s, Payne often appeared in Fox's musicals opposite Alice Faye or Betty Grable. In the 1950s, his forte was westerns and action films. He retired from films in 1957 to star in his own television western series *The Restless Gun*, but briefly returned to films in the late 1960s.

Above: For his Academy Award-winning performance, Edmund Gwenn infused Kris Kringle with an air of self assurance, dignity and a sense of humor. Gwenn regarded the Oscar as a reward for his skill at comedy. When on his death bed, he was visited by his old friend George Seaton, who seeing him in pain said, 'Oh, Teddy, it must be awfully hard.' 'Yes,' Gwenn gamely replied with a smile, 'but not as hard as playing comedy.'

Left: A publicity still featuring John Payne, Edmund Gwenn and Natalie Wood. No Christmas would be complete without seeing these three smiling faces at least once. Like other Christmas classics (**It's a Wonderful Life** (1946), **Going My Way** (1944) or **White Christmas** (1954) to name a few), **Miracle on 34th Street** is as much a part of the holiday season as eggnog and mistletoe. It's not surprising to hear of families or friends who plan an evening around watching the film. Though they may have seen it dozens of times before, everyone will gather round the television and recite the characters' lines right along with them. A childhood favorite of many, **Miracle on 34th Street** is like a beloved book that parents want to share with their children.

Facing page: In this behind-the-scenes shot, Edmund Gwenn and John Payne help Natalie Wood rehearse for her piano playing scene.

Overleaf: Susan reluctantly gives Kris the chance to prove that he really is Santa Claus by telling him what she wants for Christmas. She shows him a page torn from a magazine—a picture of a house in the suburbs. He assumes she wants a doll house, but what she wants is a real house with a backyard and a great big tree with a swing. When he indicates that her request may be somewhat hard to deliver, her skepticism returns:

'If you're really Santa Claus, you can get it for me and if you can't then you are only a nice man with a white beard like Mother said.'

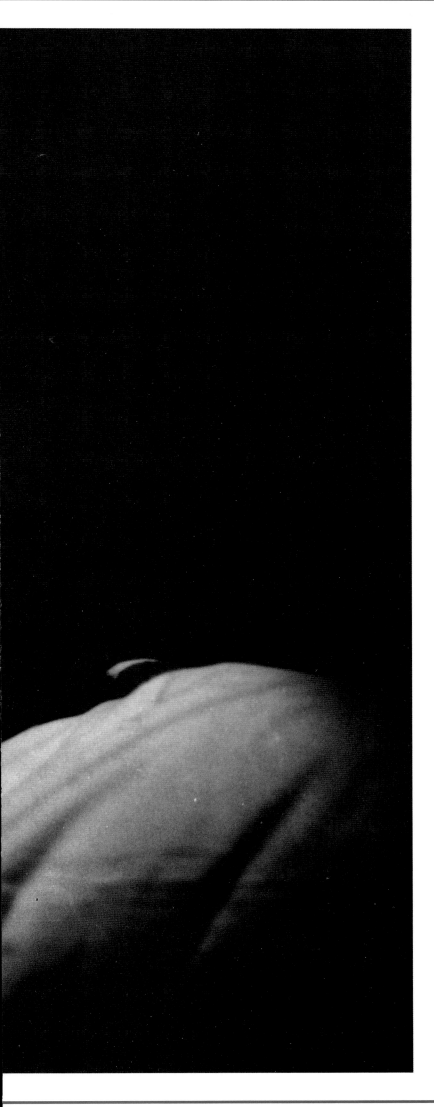

Left: Promising to see what he can do about her unusual request, Kris kisses Susan good night. 'It's a tall order but I'll do my best.' Having noticed Fred's interest in Mrs Walker, Kris sees how Fred may play a part in realizing Susie's dream house and encourages him to ask Doris out to dinner or the theater.

56

Left: Kris perseveres in his mission to convert Susie. In this scene, Kris sings her a good night song: 'To market, to market to buy a fat pig. Home again, home again, jiggity jig.'

He interrupts his song to watch Susan blow bubble gum. Still a child at heart, he asks to try some bubble gum himself. The camera zooms in on Susan's face as her eyes widen with amazement and then clench shut as we hear the sound of a bubble bursting. She opens one eye to assess the situation and, seeing the damage, closes it again. The scene fades away to Kris plucking bubble gum out of his beard.

Facing page: In this scene, which was cut from the final film version, Susan practices her newly found skills for playing make believe. Pretending to be a caged animal, Susan mugs for the camera. Natalie Wood played Susan with a naturalness rarely found in child actors.

Director George Seaton decided this scene was unnecessary, as the earlier scene in which Edmund Gwenn as Kris teaches Susan how to be a monkey (*see* page 40) is one of the most charming in the movie. Anything more on the subject was simply overkill.

Facing page: This scene was also cut from the film. Though the portrait of Doris doing housework may have been true to life, director George Seaton must have decided that the image was inappropriate for a career woman and gave her a housekeeper instead.

Overleaf: Kris has made friends with a fellow employee at Macy's, a young janitor named Alfred (Alvin Greenman), who plays Santa at the local YMCA. Mr Sawyer, the store's self-appointed psychologist, has been meddling and has convinced Alfred that he plays Santa because of a guilt complex and that he hates his father—something Alfred never knew until Sawyer told him.

    Kris is angered by Sawyer's misuse of authority and confronts him about Alfred. Their discussion grows heated, and Kris bops him on the head with an umbrella, thereby giving Sawyer the opportunity to prove to Mrs Walker that he was right about Kris' 'latent maniacal tendencies.' Without her knowledge, Sawyer whisks Kris off to Bellevue, New York's city hospital with its infamous ward for the insane.

Left: This scene, which never made it to the final cut, shows Kris being interviewed by a doctor at Bellevue. In the film, the audience learns through Fred that Kris, depressed because he thinks Doris has betrayed him, has deliberately failed the mental exam.

Kris is now a captive in the state system and faces being committed. Fred must come to his rescue and request a formal hearing before a judge who will determine Kris' sanity.

Again Seaton uses irony to make a point, having Kris Kringle point out that it is a crazy world if people like Sawyer are considered normal, while nice people like him are locked up in insane asylums.

Mr Macy is outraged by Mr Sawyer's actions and tells him that he wants the case against Kris Kringle dropped. Wanting to avoid undue publicity for Macy's, Mr Sawyer seeks out Fred (*facing page*) and unwittingly gives him the perfect idea for defending Kris Kringle — publicity and lots of it. If he is to win the case, Fred needs public opinion on his side. Soon the newspapers are filled with sympathetic stories about Santa on trial for lunacy.

Porter Hall played the part of Mr Sawyer. A character actor known for his portrayals of sneaky and spineless men, Hall appeared in numerous films, including **The Petrified Forest** (1936), **Wells Fargo** (1937), **Mr Smith Goes to Washington** (1939), **His Girl Friday** (1940), **Going My Way** (1944) and **The Big Carnival** (1951).

Left: It is up to Judge Henry X Harper to decide whether or not Kris Kringle is insane. Everyone knows there is no such person as Santa Claus. Therefore, Kris Kringle must be insane. The judge is up for re-election and this case doesn't help his campaign. In fact, declaring Kris Kringle insane will be political suicide for his career. He'll be remembered as the man who locked up Santa Claus. The judge is an honest man who takes his job seriously and is only doing his duty. However, his political advisor, Charlie (William Frawley), recommends that he take a vacation and avoid the case. The judge finally understands the political implications of declaring Santa Claus a lunatic when his grandchildren refuse to hug him good night. When asked to rule on the existence of Santa Claus, the judge wisely declares that the court will keep an open mind.

Judge Henry Harper was smoothly played by Gene Lockhart, a veteran vaudeville, stage and film actor. Equally at home playing good guys or bad, he starred in some 100 films, including **A Christmas Carol** (1938), **Abe Lincoln in Illinois** (1940), **They Died With Their Boots On** (1942), **Joan of Arc** (1948), **Madame Bovary** (1949), **Carousel** (1956) and **Jeanne Eagels** (1957).

Overleaf: Like the judge, Fred faces a difficult task. He must prove that Kris Kringle *is* Santa Claus.

Right: Kris Kringle is called to the stand.

'What is your name?' the prosecutor asks.

'Kris Kringle.'

'Where do you live?'

'That's what this hearing will decide,' says Kris with a twinkle in is eye.

'Do you believe that you are Santa Claus?'

'Of course.'

'The state rests, your honor.'

The part of Thomas Mara, the prosecutor, was played by Jerome Cowan, who is perhaps best known for his performance as Miles Archer in **The Maltese Falcon** (1941). Cowan's easy-going yet polished manner made him a natural as a supporting actor. Typically urbane and intelligent, and often sporting a pencil-thin mustache, he starred in over 100 films, including **Beloved Enemy** (1936, his first film), **The Goldwyn Follies** (1938), **High Sierra** (1941), **Song of Bernadette** (1943), **The Fountainhead** (1948), **Young Man with a Horn** (1950), **Visit to a Small Planet** (1960) and **The Gnome Mobile** (1961).

Facing page: Charlie, the judge's political advisor, was played by veteran character actor William Frawley. From his vantage point in the court room, Charlie makes his opinion known to the judge by jabbing the air with his ever-present cigar.

Known to television fans around the world as Fred Mertz from the long running 'I Love Lucy' series, William Frawley began his career in vaudeville. Once in Hollywood he appeared in roughly 150 films, including **Footsteps in the Dark** (1941) with Errol Flynn, **Going My Way** (1944) with Bing Crosby and **Rancho Notorious** (1952) with Marlene Dietrich. True to his comedic roots, Frawley played an ornery but likeable character as he did in **Miracle on 34th Street**. His roles included a taxi driver, a private detective, a comic gangster and a bumbling police officer. William Frawley died in 1966.

The scene depicted *at right* highlights the conflict between the leading romantic figures. Fred represents idealism, while Doris stands for hard-nosed practicality. Feeling the flush of success from his day in court, Fred has rushed to meet Doris. She can't believe he is serious. He'll be branded a lunatic himself and will jeopardize his career if he attempts to prove Kris Kringle is really Santa Claus. He tells her he has quit his job and that she just needs to have faith in him, but she tells him:

   'It's not a question of faith. It's just common sense.' To which he replies, 'Faith is believing in things when common sense tells you not to,' a line that sums up the central theme of the film. Kris Kringle symbolizes the ultimate leap of faith. Doris (and the audience as well) must have what literary critics refer to as a 'willing suspension of disbelief' if she is to believe in Santa Claus or any other myth, fairy tale or legend.

Right: Fred points out that 'It's not just Kris that's on trial. It's everything that he stands for. It's kindness and joy and love, and all the other intangibles....They are the only things that are worthwhile.' But to Doris, Fred has gone on an 'idealistic binge.'

   To emphasize the rift between Doris and Fred, in the final film version director George Seaton had John Payne leave his coat on throughout the scene.

Left: In this delightful scene, Thomas Mara Jr, the prosecutor's son, is called to the stand. Tommy testifies that Santa Claus is in the courtroom and, more importantly, that he knows there is a Santa Claus because his daddy told him so. Following Tommy's testimony, the state concedes the existence of Santa Claus, but calls for the defense to produce authoritative proof that Kris Kringle is the one and only Santa Claus. The judge agrees that the defense must produce authoritative proof and adjourns court for day.

Facing page: Like the characters they played on screen, Natalie Wood and John Payne had a good relationship off screen. Here, he helps her learn her lines.

When not working on a film, Natalie Wood attended school at the studio. Her life and that of her family was dominated by the studio. Her sister Lana, who was born in 1947, the year **Miracle on 34th Street** was released, would also attend the studio's school. Natalie's father worked at the studio, first as a carpenter and then in the special effects department, and her mother, the driving force behind Natalie's career, was always by her side when a film was being made.

Facing page: One of the difficulties of being a child actress is maintaining a semblance of ordinary life. With the assistance of her co-star John Payne, Natalie Wood takes a turn around the lot at 20th Century-Fox Studios on her new two-wheeler.

A good portion of **Miracle on 34th Street** was filmed on location in New York, but as the palm tree in the background suggests the cast and crew were obviously back in Hollywood.

Facing page: Although this scene was cut from the final version of the film, it illustrates one of the reasons behind the film's success: Maureen O'Hara and Natalie Wood made a convincing portrait of mother and daughter. The two clearly have a good relationship. A single parent, Doris has brought Susie up in a loving environment and Susie is a polite, charming little girl. The Catholic Church, however, did not approve of the leading character being a divorced woman and, declaring it morally objectionable, gave it a 'B' rating.

Overleaf: This scene typifies what makes **Miracle on 34th Street** such a wonderful film. Watching Doris and Susie together makes us feel good. After court is adjourned for the day, Doris goes home to Susie and tries to explain what is happening. As they cuddle up in the chair, Susie tells her mother that Kris Kringle must be Santa — 'He's so nice and kind and jolly; he's not like anyone else.' We can tell that Doris is softening and that she too is beginning to share Susie's feelings. This scene climaxes in Susie's decision to write a letter to Kris Kringle to cheer him up. She tells him that she believes in him and Doris adds a postscript that she believes too. Susie addresses the letter to Kris at the court house, which inspires a postal worker to send *all* the letters to Santa to the court house.

Left: To Kris Kringle, Doris and Susie are 'the whole thing in miniature.' They represent a 'test case' in his struggle to keep the true meaning of Christmas alive. 'Christmas isn't just a day,' he explains. 'It's a frame of mind. If I can win you over, there's still hope,' he tells her. 'If not, then I guess I'm through.' As this scene reveals, Kris was able to win them over.

Right: This is another scene that never made it to the final print of the movie. Susie's anguish was out of step with the tenor of the film and was later cut.

Though Hollywood jargon refers to scenes 'left on the cutting room floor' in reality out-takes such as this one are carefully cataloged for possible future inclusion in the film. On rare occasions, out-takes are restored to a film after its original release, though more often than not they are consigned to a bin where they provide an interesting chronology of the making of a film.

Thanks to Susie's letter to Kris Kringle, Fred found the authoritative proof he needed to win the case. Armed with three letters addressed to Santa Claus and delivered to Kris, Fred makes the point that the post office—a branch of the United States government—recognizes Kris Kringle as the one and only Santa Claus. When the District Attorney objects that three letters are hardly proof, Fred volunteers that he has more proof but is hesitant to bring it into the courtroom. 'Put them here on my desk,' the judge insists in one of the film's most memorable lines. Moments later the judge is buried under hundred of letters to Santa Claus. Camera bulbs flash (*left*) as the judge declares the case dismissed.

Left: It is Christmas Day and the air crackles with expectation. Kris Kringle has invited Fred, Doris and Susan to join him in celebrating Christmas Day at the Brooks Memorial Home, where he lives.

Overleaf: Susan dashes to the Christmas tree and is disappointed that she didn't get what she asked for for Christmas. Having learned a valuable lesson from Kris, Doris tries to console her, telling her 'Just because things don't turn out the way you want them to the first time, you've still got to believe.'

Right: 'I don't suppose you even want to talk to me ... I'm sorry, Susie. I tried my best.' With this scene, director George Seaton sets us up for the happy conclusion.

George Seaton began his career as a stage actor and producer, turning to films in 1933, first as a screenwriter and later as a director. He continued to write screenplays, however, and was quite successful at it, earning Academy Awards for his screenplays for **Miracle on 34th Street** and **The Country Girl** (1952). In the early 1950s he formed a partnership with William Perlberg, producer of **Miracle on 34th Street**, and produced several films with him over the next decade. Seaton's directorial credits include **Chicken Every Sunday** (1949), **The Proud and the Profane** (1956), **Teacher's Pet** (1958), **The Pleasure of His Company** (1961), **36 Hours** (1965) and **Airport** (1970). Along with Perlberg, he produced **Somebody Loves Me** (1952) and **The Bridges at Toko-Ri** (1955), among others. Seaton also wrote the screenplay for **Song of Bernadette** (1943), which interestingly enough is another film that deals with faith and miracles.

Right: Now converted to Kris' way of thinking, Doris bids Kris good-bye as this heart-warming story nears its conclusion. In Britain, the film was released as **The Big Heart**.

In addition to Academy Awards for George Seaton (Best Screenplay) and Edmund Gwenn (Best Supporting Actor), the film garnered Valentine Davies an Oscar for Best Original Story. Born and raised in New York City, the setting for **Miracle on 34th Street**, Davies was a playwright and novelist before he began writing for the screen in 1941. A friend of George Seaton, Davies collaborated with him on **Chicken Every Sunday** (1949) and **The Bridges at Toko-Ri** (1955). **Chicken Every Sunday** was part of a bargain made with Darryl F Zanuck, production chief at 20th Century-Fox. If Davies and Seaton would do **Chicken Every Sunday**, the studio would produce **Miracle on the 34th Street**. Valentine Davies also wrote and directed **The Benny Goodman Story** (1955).

Right: It still is Christmas Day and Kris Kringle has a little magic yet to work. Kris gives Fred directions for a short cut back to the city, and on the way home, Susie suddenly screams 'Stop, Uncle Fred! Stop!' Jumping from the car, she runs into a house, with Fred and Doris in pursuit.

Left: 'This is my house, Mommy. The one I asked Mr Kringle for. It is. It is,' Susan explains excitedly to a dazed Doris and Fred.

In this climactic scene, Fred realizes that Doris does believe in him. Conveniently, the house is for sale. They look each other and decide they want to get married — and not just to keep Susie from being disappointed. Suddenly, Fred's attention — along with that of the audience — is drawn to the corner of room, where a cane, just like the one Kris Kringle always carried, is leaning against the wall. As the credits begin to roll, we all begin to think that maybe there really is a Santa Claus.

Above: Studios were often fond of staging publicity shots for the leading characters. In this shot John Payne and Maureen O'Hara feign confusion, while Edmund Gwenn acts oblivious as he talks on the phone.

Above: Another publicity shot from the same shooting. Iron-
ically, the studio lost the biggest publicity boost it could
have had by not releasing the movie during the Christmas
season. Instead, **Miracle on 34th Street** was released in
June 1947.

Facing page: John Payne and Maureen O'Hara pose for the obligatory shot of the romantic leads. Some critics felt that Payne and O'Hara were ill suited for the leads, that he lacked animation and she warmth. In reality, both were perfect. Their love story had to be secondary to the main plot, with the focus on Edmund Gwenn, the real star of the show, and Natalie Wood.

Although **Miracle on 34th Street** may be overlooked by serious critics, it is a truly wonderful film. Filled with humor and irony, it is entertaining as well as uplifting and carries with it a timeless message. We would all do well to be a little bit more like Kris Kringle whatever the time of year.

INDEX